Building Social Relationships

Building Social Relationships:

A Systematic Approach to Teaching Social Interaction Skills to Children and Adolescents With Autism Spectrum Disorders and Other Social Difficulties

INSTRUCTOR MANUAL

Scott Bellini, Ph.D.

AAPC Textbooks
A Division of

Autism Asperger Publishing Co.
P.O. Box 23173
Shawnee Mission, Kansas 66283-0173
www.aapctextbooks.net

© 2008 Autism Asperger Publishing Co.
P.O. Box 23173
Shawnee Mission, Kansas 66283-0173
www.aapctextbooks.net

All rights reserved. With the exception of the contents on the accompanying CD, which may be used and modified by the instructor, no part of the material protected by this copyright notice may be reproduced or used in any form or by any means, electronic or mechanical, including photocopying, recording, or by any information storage and retrieval system, without the prior written permission of the copyright owner.

Publisher's Cataloging-in-Publication

Bellini, Scott.
Building social relationships : a systematic approach to teaching social interaction skills to children and adolescents with autism spectrum disorders and other social difficulties instructor manual / Scott Bellini. -- 1st ed.– Shawnee Mission, KS : Autism Asperger Pub. Co., 2008.

   p. ; cm. + 1 CD-ROM (4 3/4 in.)

   ISBN-13: 978-1-934575-04-8
   Accompanied by CD-ROM which contains chapter PowerPoint presentations, chapter tests and a comprehensive exam.
   Accompanies: Building social relationships: a systematic approach to teaching social interaction skills to children and adolescents with autism spectrum disorders and other social difficulties.

   1. Social interaction in children--Study and teaching--Handbooks, manuals, etc. 2. Social interaction in adolescence--Study and teaching--Handbooks, manuals, etc. 3. Social skills in children--Study and teaching--Handbooks, manuals, etc. 4. Social skills--Study and teaching--Handbooks, manuals, etc. 5. Communicative disorders in children--Study and teaching--Handbooks, manuals, etc. 6. Communicative disorders in adolescence--Study and teaching--Handbooks, manuals, etc. I. Title. II. Building social relationships: a systematic approach to teaching social interaction skills to children and adolescents with autism spectrum disorders and other social difficulties.

RJ506.A9 B45 2007
618.92/85882--dc22   0708

Designed in Lucida Sans.

Printed in the United States of America.

Table of Contents

Introduction 1

Overview of Features: Instructor Manual 5

Overview of Features: Textbook 7

Chapter Summaries 9

Preparing for Your Class:
    Recommended Case Studies and In-Class Activities 19

Project Ideas 29

Paper Topic Ideas 36

References 41

Introduction

Since the publication of the original version of *Building of Social Relationships* in July of 2006, I have had the opportunity to conduct a meta-analysis of 55 social skill intervention studies for children and adolescents with autism spectrum disorders (ASD) (Bellini, Peters, Benner, & Hopf, 2006). The results were sobering, if not surprising. The study revealed that social skill interventions are only minimally effective for children with ASD. These results are consistent with the dismal findings of previous meta-analyses of social skill interventions with other populations of children (Gresham, Sugai, & Horner, 2001; Quinn, Kavale, Mathur, Rutherford, & Forness, 1999). Such findings can lead us down two different paths: (a) quit now and cut our losses, or (b) commit ourselves to developing more effective social skills interventions. I have chosen the latter path, and this textbook reflects that decision.

As stated in the introduction to the textbook, we do not necessarily need more social skills programming, we need *better* social skills programming. The results of the meta-analyses, though hard to swallow, shed some light on factors that lead to more beneficial social outcomes for children with ASD and other populations of children. For instance, by synthesizing the results of meta-analyses, we are better able to determine the ingredients of effective social skills instruction and, thus, make recommendations for programming. They are as follows:

1. Increase the dosage of social skill interventions.
2. Provide instruction within the child's natural setting.
3. Match the intervention strategy with the type of skill deficit demonstrated.
4. Conduct a reliable and valid social skill assessment prior to implementing strategies.
5. Develop measurable and unambiguous intervention objectives.
6. Implement direct and systematic social skills instruction.
7. Ensure intervention fidelity.

The good news is that information on each of these recommendations for effective programming is contained within this textbook.

Building Social Relationships was originally written as a "translational text." That is, my goal was to translate a conceptual model into an intervention manual that would be understandable and meaningful to practitioners from a wide range of disciplines. As I began the writing process, I realized that it would be most beneficial to write the book in a style that would be understandable to parents as well. After all, parents often find themselves shouldering much of the responsibility regarding implementation of social skills programming. The result is a book that is built upon a conceptual foundation, but is also filled with a large collection of effective strategies. I believe that the style and content incorporated in this textbook will be appealing to your students. I also believe that *Building Social Relationships* is a book that they will keep on their shelves for future reference and use.

Soon after publication, I began to receive correspondence from college instructors across the country expressing their interest in using *Building Social Relationships* in their courses. As a researcher, clinician, and college instructor, the conversion of *Building Social Relationships* into a textbook seemed to me like the logical next step. In fact, until the textbook version was created, I used the original version as the text in my own course on social skills training. I found that the five-step model outlined in the original text provides a wonderful framework for structuring and organizing the course. I am confident that this textbook version of *Building Social Relationships*, with its many added features, will be even more useful to instructors teaching courses related to social skills training.

Many of the instructors who have contacted me teach courses on social skills training that are not disability specific. Their primary question/comment is whether my social skills model, and thus the book, can be applied to other populations of children. My answer to them is the same as my answer to the hundreds of practitioners and parents who have contacted me in the last year with similar questions, YES! Though I created the systematic, five-step model to specifically address the extensive social needs of children with ASD, it can be useful and effective with other populations as well.

For those of you wishing to use *Building Social Relationships* in a social skills training course that is not specific to ASD (which, incidentally, is what I do), I suggest that you omit Chapter 3, which provides a detailed description of the social behaviors of children with ASD. This section may be replaced with a general description of social skills, or with a description of the social functioning of the population you are addressing (e.g., attention deficit/hyperactivity disorder, emotional disorders). If you are teaching a class with students from a diverse range of disciplines, you may have them accumulate lists of social skills and skill deficits from populations of children that are of most interest to them, and then compare and contrast the students' findings. As they compare and contrast the social skills of children from various populations, many more similarities than differences will likely emerge. The important thing is that your students be able to identify social skills that lead to social success and/or social skill deficits that lead to social failure.

Finally, though the intervention strategies presented in Chapters 8 and 9 are broad and extensive, there are many other social skills strategies available to researchers and practitioners. My suggestion is to have your students conduct literature searches for other strategies. Again, the goal of every student should be to expand his or her intervention tool chest. The model presented in this textbook provides ample room for the inclusion of additional strategies. As students find strategies not covered in the textbook, have them answer the questions posed in Chapter 7 under the heading "Questions to Answer When Selecting Intervention Strategies."

Of course, these recommendations (and others presented in this Instructor Manual) for incorporating *Building Social Relationships* into your course on social skill training are merely suggestions. You will make the ultimate decisions regarding course content and instructional style. I hope that you find the content and structure of the textbook useful in organizing, structuring, and teaching your course. And perhaps most important, I hope that you and your students will find the book to be as enjoyable to read as it was for me to write.

Overview of Features: Instructor Manual

This Instructor Manual serves as a companion to the textbook, *Building Social Relationships*, and includes the following features for instructors' use:

- **Chapter summaries** – Recall the main points of each chapter as a refresher prior to reviewing case study reminders, recommendations for in-class activities, project ideas, paper ideas, Power Point™ presentations, chapter tests, and the comprehensive exam.

- **Case study reminders** – Refer to the *Preparing for Your Class: Recommended Case Studies and In-Class Activities* chapter for reminders to generate case studies or real-life stories based on your professional and personal experiences, before discussing the complementary material in class. While the textbook includes case studies based on my experiences, sharing your own experiences and encouraging your students to also share theirs will greatly enhance instructor-student enthusiasm and engagement, which in turn leads to enhanced in-class discussions. Case study reminders are paired with the symbol to the right.

In This Manual

- **Recommendations for in-class activities** – Refer to the *Preparing for Your Class: Recommended Case Studies and In-Class Activities* chapter to learn suggestions for in-class activities related to each chapter. Recommendations for in-class activities are paired with the symbol shown on the left.

- **Project ideas** – Refer to the *Project Ideas* chapter for ideas that range from those appropriate for assignment at the beginning of the semester, to those to be completed over the course of the semester, or those that are relevant to a specific chapter and should be assigned either prior to or following in-class discussion of a given chapter.

- **Paper topic ideas** – Finally, the *Paper Topic Ideas* chapter outlines recommended topics for student papers.

On the Accompanying CD-Rom ...

- **Chapter Power Point™ presentations** – The CD-Rom includes text-based Power Point presentations that highlight the main points of each chapter. Instructors may add the slide design of their choice to each presentation. Power Point slides are reproducible for educational purposes in your course only.

- **Chapter tests** – The CD-Rom includes a printable test for each chapter. Instructors may modify these as they wish. These may be shared with students (a) as a self-check of their knowledge and understanding of a chapter's material, (b) as a study guide, or (c) as an in-class test or quiz. Tests are reproducible for educational purposes in your course only.

- **Comprehensive Exam** – The CD-Rom includes a comprehensive exam. The exam largely includes short-answer questions designed to evaluate students' overall understanding of the material that comprises the Five-Step Model for Social Skills Programming presented in this textbook. Instructors may modify the exam as they wish. The exam may be reproduced for educational purposes in your course only.

Overview of Features: Textbook

The *Building Social Relationships* textbook contains the following features to help students strengthen their understanding of material discussed within each chapter, as well as share this knowledge with parents and colleagues and apply it to their everyday work with children and adolescents with ASD:

- **Chapter learner objectives** – Refer to the list of learner objectives at the beginning of each chapter for a preview of the chapter's content, as well as to learn what information you are expected to understand and be able to explain after reading the chapter.

- **Vocabulary** – Note the terms included in grey boldface text within each chapter for at-a-glance reminders of key vocabulary. The definitions for these terms are included in the glossary in Appendix C.

- **Chapter summary** – Review the main points listed at the end of each chapter to recall the main points discussed within the chapter.

- **Chapter review questions** – Answer the questions at the end of each chapter to check your understanding of and ability to explain the information discussed within the chapter. The review questions may also be used as a study guide when preparing for tests and/or exams.

- **Chapter review answers** – Refer to Appendix B to confirm your answers to the review questions that accompany each chapter.

- **Glossary** – Refer to Appendix C for an alphabetical listing of all vocabulary terms included in grey boldface text within the textbook (as previously mentioned).

Table 1 provides a summary and comparison of the contents of the Instructor Manual and textbook features.

Table 1

Feature	Instructor Manual	Textbook
Chapter Learner Objectives		X
Chapter Power Point™ Presentations	X – CD-Rom	
Case Study Reminders	X	
Recommendations for In-Class Activities	X	
Chapter Summary	X	X
Chapter Review Questions		X
Chapter Review Answers		X
Chapter Tests	X – CD-Rom	
Glossary		X
References	X	X
Project Ideas	X	
Paper Topic Ideas	X	
Exam	X – CD-Rom	

Chapter Summaries

Introduction

This book describes a five-step model that promotes effective social skills programming by providing a conceptual framework from which professionals and parents may work. The steps included in this model are:

- *Assess Social Functioning*
- *Distinguish Between Skill Acquisition and Performance Deficits*
- *Select Intervention Strategies*
    - a. *Strategies That Promote Skill Acquisition*
    - b. *Strategies That Enhance Performance*
- *Implement Intervention*
- *Evaluate and Monitor Progress*

Chapter 1

The social skills program covered in this book is based on five fundamental tenets of social skills programming. The tenets incorporate both research on social skills programming and clinical experience.

- *Tenet #1: Individuals With ASD Want to Establish Meaningful Social Relationships.*

- *Tenet #2: If We Want Children and Adolescents With ASD to Be Successful Socially, We Must Teach Them the Skills to Be Successful.*
- *Tenet #3: Successful Social Behaviors Are Not Always Appropriate Social Behaviors.*
- *Tenet #4: Social Success Is Dependent Upon Our Ability to Adapt to Our Environment.*
- *Tenet #5: Social Interaction Skills Are Not the Equivalent of Academic Skills.*

Chapter 2

Social interactions involve three integrated components: thinking, feeling, and doing. These components do not work in isolation. Instead they work in concert, each capable of promoting or hindering successful social performance.

- **Thinking** *involves knowing what to do (declarative knowledge) and how to do it (procedural knowledge). Thinking also involves taking another person's perspective and self-awareness.*
- **Feeling** *involves regulating emotions, such as anxiety, that might otherwise hinder successful social performance.*
- **Doing** *involves the execution (e.g., motor movements) of the social performance.*

Chapter 3

The skills and deficits described in this chapter provide the context for the social skills program to be presented in the following chapters. These are the skills that we will be examining in our assessment and later targeting in our intervention.

The social skill deficits are divided into six broad categories of social impairment. It is important to note that these categories are not mutually exclusive but are interconnected. No single social skill operates in isolation of the others.

- ***Nonverbal communication skills*** *are the foundation of successful social interactions. Children with ASD often have difficulties recognizing emotions and inferring the meaning of the nonverbal communication of others.*

- ***Social initiations*** *involve joining in social activities, greetings, and asking questions, among many others. Children with ASD typically fall into one of two categories of social initiation: those who rarely initiate interactions with others and those who initiate frequently, but inappropriately.*

- ***Reciprocity and terminating interactions*** *involves the give-and-take of social interactions. Children with ASD often engage in one-sided interactions that lack the mutual, back-and-forth exchange of reciprocal interactions.*

- ***Social cognition*** *refers to the ability to process social information. Social cognition involves both social problem solving (analyzing social situations) and understanding social rules.*

- ***Perspective taking and self-awareness*** *pose difficulties for most children with ASD and lead to many of the social behaviors they typically demonstrate. These behaviors include making inappropriate comments, failure to maintain hygiene, violation of personal space, and failing to consider the interests of others.*

- ***Social anxiety and social withdrawal*** *is common in children with ASD. Social anxiety significantly hinders social performance and may lead to social withdrawal, solitary interests, and isolation.*

Chapter 4

The Five-Step Model for Social Skills Programming provides a conceptual framework for developing and implementing social skills programming and is applicable to professionals and parents. The five steps of the model include:

- Assess Social Functioning
- Distinguish Between Skill Acquisition and Performance Deficits

- *Select Intervention Strategies*
    a. *Strategies That Promote Skill Acquisition*
    b. *Strategies That Enhance Performance*
- *Implement Intervention*
- *Evaluate and Monitor Progress*

Chapter 5

A thorough social skills assessment allows parents and professionals to identify the critical skills that are hindering the child's social performance. Most important, the assessment helps us identify the skills that the child will need to be successful socially. Identification of targeted skills leads directly to the development of social objectives. That is, the social skills that we will teach to the child as part of the social skills program.

After the social skills assessment is complete, and you have identified the three to five objectives to be targeted, the next step is to determine whether the deficits can be attributed to a skill acquisition deficit or a performance deficit.

- *The social skills assessment consists of the following four components: general interview of social performance, problem identification and analysis interview, observation of social functioning, and rating forms.*

- *Whereas social goals concentrate on building new skills and represent long-term learning, social objectives define short-term behaviors and describe specific levels of performance. Objectives should be connected to the stated goals and linked directly to the intervention strategies selected.*

- *Objective criteria that are realistic and meaningful to the child should be selected. Criteria should be based on the child's present level of performance and should be updated continually based on the child's progress.*

- *In developing social objectives, it is imperative to reframe "problems" into positive, teachable skills.*

◎ *Three to five social objectives are sufficient per three-month quarter. This will allow parents and professionals to better focus their efforts on critical skill deficits, and to also target the component skills that will needed to successfully reach the social objective.*

Chapter 6

Successful social programming is dependent upon our ability to distinguish between a skill acquisition deficit and a performance deficit. A skill acquisition deficit refers to the absence of a particular skill or behavior. A performance deficit refers to a skill or behavior that is present, but not performed.

◎ *The skill acquisition/performance deficit dichotomy guides the selection of intervention strategies. Some strategies are designed to promote skill acquisition, while others are designed to enhance performance. The key to successful social skills programming is to match the type of intervention strategies with the type of skill deficit.*

◎ *Acquisition of social skills proceeds on a continuum from novice to intermediate, to mastery.*

◎ *Social performance can be negatively impacted by several factors, even after the child has reached a level of mastery with a given skill. These factors include motivation, sensory sensitivities, anxiety, attention and impulsivity, memory, self-efficacy, and movement differences.*

Chapter 7

Unfortunately, a single intervention strategy does not exist that will aid all children and adolescents with ASD in being successful socially. A combination of strategies should be used to best meet a child's needs, with an emphasis on matching intervention strategies to the type of skill deficit demonstrated (skill acquisition or performance deficit). The following six questions should be answered when selecting intervention strategies:

◎ *What specific social skills will be targeted?*

- *Does the strategy match the type of skill deficit demonstrated (for each skill)?*
- *What is the child's developmental level (language and cognitive functioning)?*
- *Is the strategy supported by research?*
- *If the strategy is not supported by research, what is the rationale/logic for using it?*
- *Which components of social interaction skills (i.e., thinking, feeling, doing) does the strategy address?*

A balance between social accommodation and social assimilation is necessary to ensure effective overall social skills programming.

Chapter 8

This chapter provided a broad collection of social skill intervention strategies designed to promote skill acquisition in children with ASD. As such, these strategies are most appropriate for teaching skills that the child does not already possess, or possesses at a novice level. Though the strategies were presented separately in the text, in many cases they may be used in combination with other strategies. In addition, some of the strategies (e.g., Social Stories™, video modeling, and prompting) can be used to promote skill acquisition AND to enhance performance. The strategies covered in this chapter included:

- *Thoughts, Feelings, and Interests*
- *Reciprocal Intervention Strategies*
- *Social Stories*
- *Role Playing/Behavioral Rehearsal*
- *Video Modeling*
- *Social Problem Solving and Social Rules*
- *Self-Monitoring*

◎ *Relaxation Techniques/Emotional Regulation*

◎ *Prompting Strategies*

◎ *Interaction/Conversation Planning*

Chapter 9

The strategies covered in this chapter are designed to enhance the performance of existing or newly learned skills. These strategies enhance performance either by addressing the factor diminishing performance (low self-efficacy, lack of motivation, inattention, impulsivity, etc.) or by providing opportunities to perform newly learned skills. Performance enhancement strategies should be used to supplement skill acquisition strategies. The performance enhancement strategies covered in this chapter include:

◎ *Reinforcement/Contingency Strategies*

◎ *Gaming Skills*

◎ *Environmental Modifications*

◎ *Peer-Mediated Instruction*

◎ *Increased Social Opportunities/Live Practice*

◎ *Disability Awareness/Peer Support Strategies*

◎ *Priming Social Behavior*

Chapter 10

This chapter provided guidelines for planning and implementing the intervention phase of the social skills program (Step 4). In addition, information was provided on conducting group social skills programming and facilitating the generalization of skills across settings and persons.

◎ *Planning the program involves determining which children will benefit, the format of the program (i.e., individual, group, or classwide), selecting peer models, training the team, selecting materials and resources, determining* where the sessions will take place, and developing a schedule.

- *Implementing the program involves effectively using play materials, connecting treatment objectives with targeted skills, introducing and teaching skills to the target child, and providing parent/teacher training and feedback to facilitate generalization.*

- *Special considerations for conducting group social skills programming include using prompts to facilitate positive social interactions between group members, withholding reinforcement until after the interaction has terminated, using play items and play themes to promote reciprocal interactions, and using free play to collect data.*

- *The generalization, or transfer, of skills to multiple settings and situations and with multiple persons is an essential aspect of social skills programming. Therefore, it is critical to develop a plan for generalization.*

Chapter 11

Accurate data collection is essential for evaluating the effectiveness of an intervention by allowing us to determine whether the child is benefiting from the instruction. If the child is not making progress, the evaluation will tell you so. Not all intervention strategies are effective for all children, and sometimes it is excruciatingly difficult to find the correct strategy for a child. However, thorough and frequent evaluations of social performance provide important information on how to modify the program to best meet the child's needs.

- *Progress monitoring involves collecting data on social functioning via observations, interviews, and rating scales.*

- *Common types of observation recording systems include frequency recording, duration recording, time sampling, latency recording, and response ratios.*

- *Interviews of parents and teachers reflect parent and teacher perceptions of progress. These interviews provide information on the appropriateness of the objectives and the strategies being implemented. This information also measures both the social validity and treatment fidelity of the intervention.*

- *Rating scales are used to provide a pre- and post-test measure of social performance. It is important to use standardized instruments with established test-retest reliability. It is also important to consider the "norm" or comparison group that was used in the standardization of the rating scale. The scores of many rating scales are based on the social performance of children without ASD. Therefore, they may not be sensitive enough to detect changes in the social performance of children with ASD.*

- *Social validity and treatment fidelity are critical to the success of a social skills program. Social validity refers to the social significance of the treatment objectives, the social significance of the intervention strategies, and the social importance of the results. Treatment fidelity refers to the degree to which the intervention was implemented as intended.*

Chapter 12

Children and adolescents with ASD often want to establish meaningful social relationships but are unable to do so due to social skill deficits and lack of effective social skills programming. Teaching social skills is a blend of science and art that incorporates methods such as:

- *Matching an intervention to the practitioner's theoretical perspective*

- *Meeting the unique needs of the child*

- *Using empirically validated/evidence-based interventions*

- *Employing creativity/ingenuity*

- *Emulating great teachers from other disciplines and fields*

In addition to incorporating this blend, practice on the part of both the child or adolescent and the instructor remains one of the most important factors in successful social skills programming.

Preparing for Your Class: Recommended Case Studies and In-Class Activities

This chapter contains recommendations for (a) case studies, or real-life stories, to be generated prior to the corresponding class sessions and (b) in-class activities, or activities that you and your students may complete and discuss during class.

Recommendations are grouped by chapter and are listed in order of the textbook material they complement. The heading for each case study reminder is preceded by the case study reminder symbol, followed in parentheses by the textbook page number with which it corresponds.

Similarly, the heading for each in-class activity is preceded by the corresponding symbol, followed in parentheses by the textbook page number with which it corresponds.

Introduction

In-Class Activity (page 3)

Provide students with 20 minutes to visit an area of the building/campus where social interactions may be observed. Ask students to select one place to sit for the duration of their observation. Have them keep a list of each social interaction they observe, the number of people involved, and the social skills that occur within each. Also ask them to consider similarities and differences between the social interactions. For example, did a group of 50-year-old-plus individuals interact with each other any differently than a group of individuals in their 20s?

When students reconvene in the classroom, use their observations as the basis for a discussion about the definition of "social skills," the myriad components involved in social skills, the factors that may affect what is deemed "typical" or "socially appropriate," and so forth. (This may also be assigned as on out-of-class project.)

Case Study Reminder (page 6)

Share examples of children and adolescents with whom you have worked on social skills or completed research. What factors did you find to be most effective in strengthening their social skills? Least effective?

Chapter 1

Case Study Reminder (page 11)

For each tenet, share an example of a child or adolescent with whom you worked on social skills or completed research, focusing on how the child or adolescent embodied the concepts described in the tenet and how that guided their social skills programming.

Chapter 2

In-Class Activity (page 23)

Demonstrate the concept of theory of mind by asking for two volunteers. With both volunteers present, hide an object in the classroom. Now ask one of the volunteers to leave the room. Move the hidden object to a new location (still out of sight). Tell the volunteer in the classroom that you are going to bring back the volunteer who left. Then ask, "When she comes back and I ask her where I hid (insert name of object), what answer will she give me?" Call the volunteer who left the room to come back and ask, "Where is the (insert name of object)?"

Discuss the difference between how the volunteer who remained in the classroom answered the question (i.e., named the location where the volunteer who left the room saw the object being hidden) and how an individual with ASD who experiences difficulty with theory of mind would answer the same question (i.e., named the location to which he saw the instructor move the item, because if he knows it has been moved, he reasons, so must the person who left the room).

Case Study Reminder (page 23)

Share an example(s) of the challenges related to theory of mind/perspective taking experienced by a child or adolescent with ASD whom you know.

Case Study Reminder (page 28)

Share an example(s) of the challenges related to anxiety experienced by a child or adolescent with ASD whom you know and how it impacted (or could have impacted) their social skills programming.

Case Study Reminder (page 30)

Share examples of challenges related to "doing," as experienced by children or adolescents with ASD with whom you have worked or conducted research.

In-Class Activity (page 32)

Have students revisit the observation notes they collected for the introductory in-class activity. Have them work in teams to select one of the social interactions. Then ask them to identify how thinking, feeling, and doing integrated to lead to a positive experience for everyone involved in the situation.

Chapter 3

Case Study Reminder (page 35)

For each category of common social skills difficulties associated with ASD, share an example(s) of a child or adolescent with whom you worked on social skills or completed research. Describe the difficulties they experienced related to the category and the impact (or in retrospect, what should have been the impact) on the child's or adolescent's social skills programming.

In-Class Activity (page 37)

Brainstorm with the class examples of nonverbal communication skills.

In-Class Activity (page 39)

Brainstorm with the class examples of social initiation skills.

In-Class Activity (page 41)

Brainstorm with the class examples of skills related to reciprocity and terminating interactions.

In-Class Activity (page 43)

Brainstorm with the class examples of social cognition skills.

In-Class Activity (page 47)

Brainstorm with the class examples of behaviors related to perspective taking and self-awareness skills.

In-Class Activity (page 50)

Brainstorm with the class examples of behaviors associated with social anxiety and withdrawal.

In-Class Activity (page 51)

Instruct your class that you are going to give them 20 minutes for a working break (to discuss or work on class-related activities). Tell them you would like half the class to take their working break in the classroom and the other half to take it in another location of your choosing (e.g., student lounge, hallway, empty classroom next door). Have the students who leave the classroom complete a working break

22 ▪ Building Social Relationships – Instructor Manual

as you described it. Have the students who remained in the classroom complete a working break of a different sort.

Divide the students in the classroom into teams of 2-3 people. Instruct each team to devise their own social culture, or ways of interacting with each other (e.g., methods of nonverbal communication, ways to initiate social interactions, ways to end social interactions, nonsense terms that will be used as if they are jokes or punch lines, unwritten rules of social behavior). For example, teams may decide to (a) give each other a high-five every time they want a turn to talk, (b) declare, "The blue balloon is delicious" and laugh heartily as though delivering a punch line to a joke, (c) touch their nose to indicate that something is interesting, and (d) turn their back to indicate that something is boring. Have the teams practice interacting with each other using the social culture they have created and tell them to use this social culture when class resumes and you provide the instruction for groups to talk about what they plan to do this weekend.

When the half of the students who left the room for the working break return, tell them that your next activity will be a group activity and that you already divided the other half of the class into groups. Ask 2-3 students to join each of the existing teams. Instruct the groups that for this activity you would like them to talk about their plans for the weekend for the next five minutes, taking mental note of all the social skills involved in this simple interaction. When the teams begin talking, you should observe one half of each group implementing their social culture and the other half attempting to be a part of the social culture/interactions, but more likely trying to figure out what exactly is occurring.

After approximately five minutes, ask the class to regroup and debrief. What did the people who took their working break outside of the classroom experience and feel during this activity? How did it impact their ability to interact with their classmates? How is this similar to what individuals with ASD may experience and how they may feel when interacting with neurotypical people? What did the students who created the new social cultures experience and how did they feel? For example, did they modify any of their behaviors to make it easier for those who did not understand the culture to join in social interactions? How is this similar to what neurotypicals may experience, or should consider, when interacting with individuals with ASD? Discuss the implications of this activity for social skills programming.

Chapter 4

Case Study Reminder (page 54)

Discuss with students how children and adolescents with ASD with whom you have worked have benefited from one or more of the steps involved in the Five-Step Model for Social Skills Programming. Likewise, share examples of how children and adolescents with ASD with whom you have worked might have benefited from implementation of this comprehensive model.

Chapter 5

In-Class Activity (page 59)

As you discuss the different methods recommended for assessment, have students share the advantages and any disadvantages associated with each.

Case Study Reminder (page 60)

Share with students an example of an interview(s) you conducted with a child or adolescent with ASD. What did you observe? What types of information did you obtain?

In-Class Activity (page 72)

Bring to class blank copies of the rating scales mentioned in Chapter 5. Make them available to students for review during a break time(s).

In-Class Activity (page 75)

Spend time with students reviewing the Autism Social Skills Profile (see textbook, pages 77-81) and Social Skills Checklist (Quill, 2000). Discuss any advantages and disadvantages associated with each. The purpose of this exercise is to strengthen students' familiarity with these ASD-specific assessment tools.

24 ▪ Building Social Relationships – Instructor Manual

Case Study Reminder and In-Class Activity (page 93)

Have students work in teams and provide each team with an IEP (black out all identifying information to maintain the child's and family's confidentiality). Ask students to critique a set of goals and objectives within the IEP based on the criteria discussed in Chapter 5. As a class, then share examples of goals and objectives that meet and do not meet the criteria.

In-Class Activity (page 93)

Have students work in teams to write an example of one social goal and its related objectives for a fictional child or adolescent with ASD. (You may have them use the stems on the Autism Social Skills Profile as objectives.) Have students describe the main characteristics/needs of the child or adolescent with ASD and share their goal and objectives with the class. Invite students to provide each other with feedback (positive comments as well as suggestions for improvement).

Chapter 6

In-Class Activity (page 104)

Have students work in teams, spending the first 10 minutes of the activity writing a list of five social skill deficits that include examples of both skill acquisition deficits and performance deficits. At the end of this time period, have teams swap their lists with each other. Teams should spend the next 10 minutes determining whether each social skill deficit listed is a skill acquisition deficit or a performance deficit. Regroup and share some of the social skills deficits and their resulting classifications.

In-Class Activity (page 107)

Ask students to identify the characteristics of each stage of skill acquisition: Novice, Intermediate, and Mastery.

Case Study Reminder and In-Class Activity (page 109)

Share with students examples of three children or adolescents with whom you have worked or completed research related to a single skill. Provide an example of one student at the Novice stage of skill acquisition, one at the Intermediate stage, and one at the Mastery Stage. Have students make a list of three skills that they perform at each of the three skill levels, for a total of nine skills.

Case Studies and In-Class Activities ▪ 25

Case Study Reminder (page 111)

Share with students real-life examples related to each of the factors that may affect social performance. Describe specifically how the factor impacted the child or adolescent with ASD and how it was (or in retrospect, should have been) addressed in the child's or adolescent's social skills programming.

Chapter 7

In-Class Activity (page 124)

Provide students with examples of strategies that promote skill acquisition and/or enhance social performance. For each, ask students to identify to which type(s) of skill deficit it may be matched.

Case Study Reminder (page 126)

Share with students an example of how you helped develop programming for a child or adolescent with ASD that balanced social accommodation and social assimilation.

Chapter 8

Case Study Reminder and In-Class Activity (page 129)

Two weeks prior to discussing Chapter 8 in class, ask students to collect examples (from their current or previous work or classes) of strategies used to promote skill acquisition in children or adolescents with ASD. (To ensure that you obtain at least one example of each strategy outlined in Chapter 8, you may have students sign up to bring in examples of a specific strategy[ies]). Instruct students to remove all identifying information from the samples to protect confidentiality (e.g., cover or black out everything but a child's first initial) and/or obtain permission from parents to share the information with the class. Ask students to bring the examples to class the day on which you will discuss Chapter 8. Supply examples from your own work with children and adolescents with ASD as well. These examples may then be referred to/shared as real-life examples of design and implementation of the strategies discussed in class.

In-Class Activity (pages 157)

Prior to discussing Chapter 8 in class, ask students to search the Internet for photos and video clips that depict social situations and that may be used as part of the social problem-solving process (SPS) with individuals with ASD. Have students bring the results of their search (i.e., photos and video clips) to the class session during which you will discuss Chapter 8. Students may then share and discuss what they have found, with an emphasis on the sources, extent, and quality of SPS resources available on the Internet.

Chapter 9

Case Study Reminder and In-Class Activity (page 189)

Two weeks prior to discussing Chapter 9 in class, ask students to collect examples (from their current or previous work or classes) of strategies used to enhance performance in children or adolescents with ASD. (To ensure that you obtain at least one example of each strategy outlined in Chapter 9, you may have students sign up to bring in examples of a specific strategy[ies].) Instruct students to remove all identifying information from the samples to protect confidentiality (e.g., cover or black out everything but a child's first initial) and/or obtain permission from parents to share the information with the class. Ask students to bring the examples to class the day on which you will discuss Chapter 9. Supply examples from your own work with children and adolescents with ASD as well. These examples may be referred to/shared as real-life examples of design and implementation of the strategies discussed in class.

Chapter 10

In-Class Activity (page 222)

Ask students to generate a list of the advantages of each type of group composition (individual and group).

Case Study Reminder and In-Class Activity (page 237)

Share with students a videotape of a group social skills session. After viewing the session, discuss which components discussed in Chapter 10 were evident in the videotaped segment. Did the session include any components not

Case Studies and In-Class Activities ▪ 27

addressed in Chapter 10? If so, which ones? From this limited insight, did they appear to be of benefit to the children or adolescents in the group? Discuss any additional student feedback regarding the video/social skills session.

Chapter 11

Case Study Reminder and In-Class Activity (page 249)

Two weeks prior to discussing Chapter 11 in class, ask students to collect examples (from their current or previous work or classes) of methods of evaluating and monitoring the social progress of children or adolescents with ASD. (To ensure that you obtain at least one example of each strategy outlined in Chapter 11, you may have students sign up to bring in examples of a specific method). Instruct students to remove all identifying information from the samples to protect confidentiality (e.g., cover or black out everything but a child's first initial) and/or obtain permission from parents to share the information with the class. Ask students to bring the examples to class the night on which you will discuss Chapter 11. Supply examples from your own work with children and adolescents with ASD as well. These examples may be referred to/shared as real-life examples of ways to evaluate and monitor social progress.

Chapter 12

In-Class Activity (page 252)

Use video clips to demonstrate/practice the various types of recording systems discussed in Chapter 11. For example, you may wish to use the video of the group social skills session viewed for Chapter 10 and ask students to take data on the target behaviors during the free-play segment.

In-Class Activity (page 265)

Encourage a class discussion during which students share their feedback regarding the conceptual framework described in this textbook. Sample topics include strengths and limitations of the framework, how applicable it is to their work, and comparisons to other social skills programming frameworks and curricula.

Project Ideas

The project ideas included here are of two types: (a) those to be assigned at the beginning of the semester, meant to be completed during the course of the semester and (b) those to be assigned prior to or following discussion of a specific chapter or section of the book in class and that are meant to be completed over a shorter period of time. An outline of each project idea is provided. These are only ideas, the specific guidelines for each project are left to your expertise, as you best know your university's/course's requirements and your students.

Semester-Long Project

Project Idea #1: Implementation of the Five-Step Model for Social Skills Programming

Review Specifics of Project: At the beginning of the semester

Project Component Due Dates: Staggered throughout the course of the semester, to follow discussion of the relevant material in-class

Project Outline:

Have each student select a child or adolescent with whom she will implement the Five-Step Model for Social Skills Programming throughout the semester with a focus on 1-2 objectives.

After each step of the model is addressed in class, students can complete it/practice implementing it with their chosen child or adolescent.

Have students compile a portfolio that documents their work with the child or adolescent, including such items as completed assessments and forms, copies of materials used when implementing strategies, data sheets, and a reflection paper. Encourage students to provide enough detail so that others would be able to replicate their interventions.

Semester-Long Project

Project Idea #2: Research to Practice

Review Specifics of Project: At the beginning of the semester

Project Component Due Dates: Two class sessions prior to the last night of class (to allow time for photocopying); assign an earlier due date if you wish to make edits and have students incorporate them before submitting a final copy of the project.

Project Outline:

Have students work in teams to research the evidence for practices recommended in Chapters 8 and 9 (students may use the citations and references as a starting point).

Assign 1-2 strategies per team, based on the size of your class. Remember that for some strategies there is more research than for others. Avoid assigning one team two strategies for which minimal or no relevant research has been conducted and another team two strategies for which a larger amount of relevant research exists.

Have each team create a table with the following column headings: (a) Article Citation; (b) Demographics (e.g., number of subjects, age, gender); (c) Other Relevant Instruments (e.g., if an instrument or strategy other than the one the team is researching has been incorporated in the study); and (d) Results. Teams should include the name of their strategy in the title of their table (e.g., Research on Prompting).

For each research study the teams find for their strategy, have them enter the relevant information on their table. If the team cannot locate any research regarding a given strategy, have them enter "No Relevant Research Located" in the first row of their table.

At the end of the semester, teams' tables may be compiled into a resource packet. Make copies of the packet, distribute them to your students, and encourage them to refer to their packets in their employment situations when searching for evidence to support a strategy(ies) they or colleagues or parents recommend using with a child.

Short-Duration Project

Project Idea #3: Social Skills-Related Rating Scales

Review Specifics of Project: At some point prior to covering the material discussed in Chapter 5

Project Due Date: The day Chapter 5 will be discussed in class

Project Outline:

Have students work in teams to review one of the rating scales described in Chapter 5 (e.g., *Social Skills Rating System*, *Behavioral Assessment Scale for Children*, *Autism Social Skills Profile*).

Have the teams present an overview of their rating scales to the class, including a handout with key information about the scale (e.g., complete citation, structure [e.g., checklist, Likert scale], purpose, target population, who can administer, standardization, main characteristics, components).

Handouts may be compiled into a resource packet for each student.

Short-Duration Project

Project Idea #4: Beyond This Book – Additional Strategies That Promote Skill Acquisition or Enhance Performance

Review Specifics of Project: At some point prior to covering the material in Chapters 8 and 9

Project Due Date: The day(s) when Chapters 8 and 9 will be discussed in class

Project Outline:

Ask students to work in teams to identify and create a list of strategies that promote skill acquisition or enhance performance, beyond those discussed in Chapters 8 and 9 of the textbook. Teams may do so by examining the research literature or searching the Internet, as well as building from their own experiences (i.e., strategies they or a colleague[s] have implemented).

Have each team select two strategies and for each, provide written answers to the six questions posed in the table on page 125: "Questions to Answer When Selecting Intervention Strategies." You may wish to review the teams' lists of strategies first and work with them to select their strategies to prevent too much overlap between teams.

In their answers to the fourth question, "Is the strategy supported by research?," teams should include a table with the following column headings: (a) Article Citation; (b) Demographics (e.g., number of subjects, age, gender); (c) Other Relevant Instruments (e.g., if an instrument or strategy other than the one their team is researching has been incorporated in the study); and (d) Results. Teams should include the name of their strategy in the title of their table (e.g., Research on Social Autopsies).

For each research study the teams find for a strategy, have them enter the relevant information on their table. If the team cannot locate any research regarding a given strategy, have them enter "No Relevant Research Located" in the first row of their table.

On the day the corresponding material is discussed in class, have teams share their two strategies and the answers to the six questions for each strategy. For instance, if a team has researched two strategies that enhance performance, have them share their findings when material from Chapter 9 is discussed in class.

At the end of the semester, teams' answers to the six questions for each strategy may be compiled into a resource packet. Make copies of the packet, distribute them to your students, and encourage them to refer to their packets in their employment situations when considering a strategy(ies) they or one of their colleagues or parents recommends using with a child.

Short-Duration Project

Project Idea #5: Practice Makes Perfect – Implementing Strategies That Promote Skill Acquisition

Review Specifics of Project: When covering material discussed in Chapter 8

Project Due Date: Per your discretion

Project Outline:

Have students implement with a child or adolescent 3-4 of the strategies described in Chapter 8 for promoting skill acquisition.

If desired, ask students to submit videotapes of their practice sessions and/or a short paper that describes the strategy practiced, includes any supporting documentation (e.g., a copy of the completed Interest Inventory, a copy of the Social Story™ used), and concludes with a reflection on factors such as advantages and disadvantages, benefits/results, and recommendations for others implementing the strategy.

Short-Duration Project

Project Idea #6: Social Skills Sessions

Review Specifics of Project: When covering material discussed in Chapter 10

Project Due Date: Per your discretion

Project Outline:

Have students implement a one-on-one social skills session and a group social skills session with children or adolescents with ASD.

If appropriate, have students work in teams to plan for and implement the group social skills session.

Have students submit a videotape of their sessions and/or a short paper that (a) describes the sessions (e.g., session schedules); (b) includes any supporting documentation (e.g., a copy of materials used, photos taken during the session); and (c) concludes with a reflection on factors such as notes about what occurred/their observations and feelings during each session, advantages and disadvantages of each type of session, and recommendations for others implementing social skills sessions.

If time and/or resources do not permit students implementing these sessions, consider having students observe a one-on-one social skills session and a group social skills session instead and submit a short paper, per the guidelines above.

Paper Topic Ideas

Paper Topic Idea #1: The Importance of Social Skills Programming for Children and Adolescents with ASD

The Assignment: Ask students to write a paper that addresses the importance of social skills programming for children and adolescents with ASD. Specifically, have students discuss aspects such as:

- Why social skills programming is a critical component of comprehensive programming for children and adolescents with AS, including: the five basic tenets of social skills programming and common areas of challenges related to social skills in children and adolescents with ASD

- The potential impact of social skills programming if (a) implemented effectively or (b) implemented poorly

- Why social skills programming is often overlooked and/or under-implemented, including any specific components of social skills programming that are often overlooked

Paper Topic Idea #2: Five-Step Model for Social Skills Programming

The Assignment: Have students write a paper that describes and identifies the importance of each step in the Five-Step Model for Social Skills Programming.

Paper Topic Idea #3: Social Skills Programming Resources: How Do They Compare?

The Assignment: Have students select two social skills programming resources (e.g., Baker, 2003; Coucouvanis, 2005; Dunn, 2006; Winner, 2005) and ask them to (a) summarize, compare, and contrast the features of each resource; and (b) evaluate them based on the guidelines for effective social skills programming included in the textbook.

Paper Topic Idea #4: When Research to Practice Isn't Possible: My Philosophy on Effective Social Skills Programming

The Assignment: Ask students to write a paper addressing the fact that minimal research exists to support social skills strategies and their beliefs regarding how to best balance using evidence-based strategies with anecdotally based (i.e., someone else told me this works), experience-based (i.e., I have found this to work), and have-a-go (i.e., let's give this a try) strategies.

Paper Topic Idea #5: The Story Behind the Data

The Assignment: Have students write a paper addressing the importance of data collection (particularly as it relates to social skills programming), various methods of data collection, and the advantages and disadvantages of each. Further, have students (a) create and describe a fictional child or adolescent (e.g., demographics, areas of strength and challenges, home and school situations); (b) select 2-3 social skills strategies they would implement with this child or adolescent; and (c) describe how and when they would collect data to monitor the child's or adolescent's progress.

References

Baker, J. E. (2003). *Social skills training for children and adolescents with Asperger Syndrome and social-communication problems.* Shawnee Mission, KS: Autism Asperger Publishing Company.

Bellini, S., Peters, J., Benner, L., & Hopf, A. (2007). A meta-analysis of school-based social skill interventions for children with autism spectrum disorders. *Remedial and Special Education, 28,* 153-162.

Coucouvanis, J. (2005). *Super skills: A social skills group program for children with Asperger Syndrome, high-functioning autism and related challenges.* Shawnee Mission, KS: Autism Asperger Publishing Company.

Dunn, M. A. (2006). *S.O.S.: Social skills in our schools.* Shawnee Mission, KS: Autism Asperger Publishing Company.

Gresham, F. M., Sugai, G., & Horner, R. H. (2001). Interpreting outcomes of social skills training for students with high-incidence disabilities. *Teaching Exceptional Children, 67,* 331-344.

Quill, K. (2000). *DO-WATCH-LISTEN-SAY: Social and communication intervention for children with autism.* Baltimore: Brookes Publishing.

Quinn, M. M., Kavale, K. A., Mathur, S. R., Rutherford Jr., R. B., & Forness, S. R. (1999). A meta-analysis of social skills interventions for students with emotional and behavioral disorders. *Journal of Emotional and Behavioral Disorders, 7,* 54-64.

Winner, M. G. (2005). *Think social!: A social thinking curriculum for school age students.* San Jose, CA: Think Social Publishing.

AAPC Textbooks

A Division of

APC

Autism Asperger Publishing Co.
P.O. Box 23173
Shawnee Mission, Kansas 66283-0173
www.aapctextbooks.net ▪ 913-897-1004